# A Selection of Early Music
from the Repertoire of the Society for Old Music

Transcribed by Audrey Ekdahl Davidson
and Published as a Tribute to Her on Her Retirement

Audrey Ekdahl Davidson in Rehearsal. Sketch by Victoria Littna, 1977.

# A Selection of Early Music

## from the Repertoire of the Society for Old Music

Transcribed by Audrey Ekdahl Davidson
and Published as a Tribute to Her on Her Retirement

Edited by Matthew Steel and Nicholas Batch

## Medieval Institute Publications

WESTERN MICHIGAN UNIVERSITY

Kalamazoo, Michigan
1993

Printed in the United States of America

ISBN 1-879288-40-0

# Contents

## Illustrations

Audrey Davidson in Rehearsal (Sketch by Victoria Littna)
The Dance of Death (Danish Wall Painting)

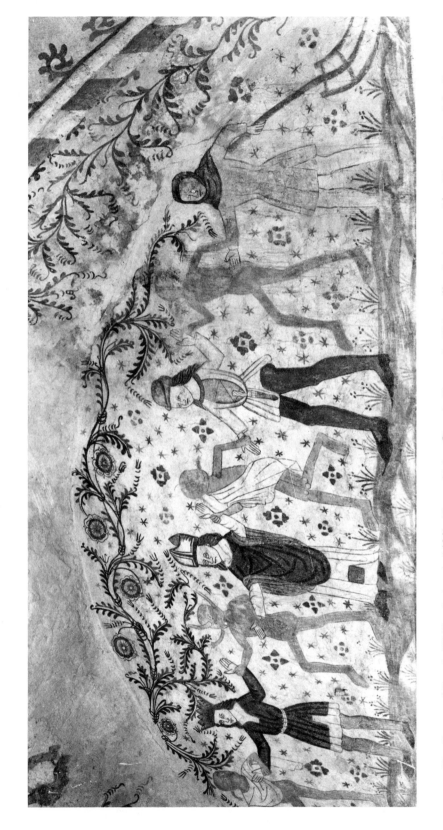

*The Dance of Death.* Wall painting (c.1480), Nørre Alslev Church, Denmark. *This wall painting provides illustration of the Dance of Death, which also formed the basis for a dance song,* Ad mortem festinamus, *No. 9, below. Courtesy of the National Museum, Copenhagen.*

# Preface

The present selection of transcriptions has been prepared for publication without Audrey Davidson's knowledge through the assistance of her husband, and has been presented to her upon the occasion of her retirement as Professor of Music at Western Michigan University. The transcriptions were all designed for performances by the Society for Old Music, which she founded in 1966 and directed until recently. Indeed, one of the examples included here, the antiphon *Alma redemptoris mater* (Sarum version), was featured at the initial concert of the Society in a performance for the Third Conference on Medieval Studies held at Western Michigan University when Davidson was a newly hired instructor in Humanities.

For a quarter of a century the Society under Davidson's direction presented a varied repertoire, including a large number of her transcriptions, many of them from early printed music books and manuscripts. The concerts of the Society were mounted for the local community, the medieval conference (which became the annual International Congress on Medieval Studies in the 1970's), and other audiences in Michigan. In 1983 the Society was invited to stage a music-drama, the Beauvais *Peregrinus*, for the International Colloquium on Medieval Drama in Viterbo, Italy. In all, the Society presented more than a dozen medieval music-dramas, including examples from Hungary and Sweden, as well as a very rare St. John Passion from Scandinavia. The most memorable, however, was the *Ordo Virtutum* of Hildegard of Bingen in 1984, and in this instance Davidson's transcription of the twelfth-century neumes became the basis for a published score that has since been widely used for other performances—e.g., by Kelly Morris' Seed and Feed Company in Atlanta which inspired the *Atlanta Journal* reviewer to exclaim that the play is "a powerful piece of musical theater."

Audrey Davidson, a native of Minnesota, received her B.A. and M.A. in music history from Wayne State University in Detroit, where she also studied with a remarkable voice teacher, Avery Crew, and had a career as a professional soprano soloist. Her Ph.D., in musicology from the University of Minnesota, culminated in the writing of a dissertation on the topic of Olivier Messiaen's Tristan Trilogy (*Harawi, Turangalîla Symphony*, and *Cinq Rechants*)—a topic which combined her love of the Middle Ages with her taste for modern music. She studied early music performance with the famed New York Pro Musica and in Europe.

As an indefatigable researcher, she ferreted out music that was exciting and often essentially unknown, as in the case of the works of Isabella Leonarda, a seventeenth-century nun from Novara, Italy, whose compositions are particularly fine. (The transcriptions of work by Isabella were done under a summer fellowship and grant from Western Michigan University, and presented in various concerts.) She spent many hours in the British Library, the Swedish Royal Archives in Stockholm, the Landesbibliothek in Wiesbaden, Germany, and other libraries abroad where she examined manuscripts and texts and made transcriptions to be used in performance.

The Society for Old Music, known for many years for its very good local singers, was never a professional group, though there was always a mix of professionals and amateurs in its makeup. Davidson, a perfectionist, always was willing to work with the available singers and instrumentalists to mold them into remarkable performances that attempted to join stylishness and excitement. Concerts ranged from medieval chant and monophonic song to polyphonic choral works by such composers as Guillaume Dufay, William Byrd, Orlando di Lasso, and Heinrich Schütz. Each concert was focused on a particular topic, most successfully perhaps on occasions when music-drama was joined to liturgical display, as in the combination of *Sponsus* and the York Corpus Christi Mass in 1976 or the revival of the *Sponsus* in its liturgical setting of Matins in 1987. *Rosa rorans*, transcribed into modern notation from square-note notation kindly supplied by Sister M. Patricia of Sankta Birgittas Kloster in Vadstena, Sweden, was one of the high points of a concert of early Scandinavian music and music-drama in 1988. In a performance of the Fleury *Raising of Lazarus* for a national music conference at the Cathedral of Christ the King in Kalamazoo in 1980, members of the audience confided that they were moved to tears at the beauty of the music and the remarkable story dramatized by the play.

The transcriptions included in the present collection are, in the view of the editors, a most fitting tribute to a colleague who has worked long, hard, and successfully in the field of early music performance. Diether Haenicke, President of Western Michigan University, provided funds for computerized typesetting of the music, a task which was done by Jeff Keefer in the computer laboratory of the School of Music. Thomas Seiler, Director of Medieval Institute Publications, not only encouraged publication but also arranged for any profits that might accrue from this collection to be designated for the support of early music. The frontispiece is a pencil drawing by the late Victoria Littna, who was a distinguished artist in her own right. We are also grateful to many others who cannot be named here for their encouragement and for helping us in various ways to make this tribute possible.

# The Publications
# of Audrey Ekdahl Davidson
# 1963–1992

"Jazz and the Tradition of Sacred Music," *Universitas: A Journal of Religion and the University*, 1 (1963), 30–37.

Translation (with Marian Johns) of text: Heinz Werner Zimmermann, *Psalm Concert*. St. Louis: Concordia, 1966.

"Milton on the Music of Henry Lawes," *Milton Newsletter*, 2 (1968), 19–23.

*I Will Sing a New Song unto the Lord: The Works of Heinz Werner Zimmermann*. Springfield, Ohio: Chantry Music Press, 1969.

"Transcendental Unity in the Works of Charles Ives," *American Quarterly*, 22 (1970), 35–44.

"Eliade and Church Renewal: The Search for the Eternal Center," *Student Musicologists at Minnesota*, 4 (1970–71), 37–75.

"The Games John Cage Plays," *Michigan Academician*, 4 (1972), 269–80.

"*Alma redemptoris mater*: The Little Clergeon's Song," *Studies in Medieval Culture*, 4 (1974), 459–66.

Review of Leslie Orrey, *A Concise History of Opera: Comparative Drama*, 9 (1975), 89–90.

*Substance and Manner: Studies in Music and the Other Arts*. St. Paul, Minn.: Hiawatha Press, 1977.

"Messiaen's Use of Peruvian Sources in his *Harawi* Song Cycle," *Michigan Academician*, 12 (1979), 47–59.

"Analogical Relationships between Music and Time," *Proceedings of the Heraclitean Society*, 4 (1979), 22–41.

"The Performance Practice of Early Music: Some Sources and Studies," *EDAM Newsletter*, 4, No. 1 (1981), 3–8.

"Olivier Messiaen's *Cinq Rechants*: The Conclusion of His Tristan Trilogy," *Centennial Review*, 25 (1981), 48-58.

(Co-author.) "The Function of Rhetoric, Marlowe's *Tamburlaine*, and 'Reciprocal Illumination'," *Ball State University Forum*, 22, No. 1 (1981), 20–29.

*The Quasi-Dramatic St. John Passions from Scandinavia and Their Medieval Background*. Kalamazoo: Medieval Institute Publications, 1981.

Review of Crown Light Editions, I–III: *EDAM Newsletter*, 5 (1983), 87–89.

"The Music and Staging of Hildegard of Bingen's *Ordo Virtutum*." In *Atti del IV Colloquio della Société Internationale pour l'Etude du Théâtre Médiéval*, ed. M. Chiabò, F. Doglio, and M. Maymone. Viterbo: Centro sul Teatro Medioevale e Rinascimentale, 1984. Pp. 495–506.

(Co-Editor.) *Sacra-Profana: Studies in Sacred and Secular Music in Honor of Johannes Riedel*. Minneapolis: Friends of Minnesota Music, 1985.

"Singing Early Music: High, Clear, and Sweet." In *Sacra/Profana: Studies in Music for Johannes Riedel*, pp. 217–26 (see above).

(Editor.) Hildegard of Bingen. *Ordo Virtutum*. Kalamazoo: Medieval Institute Publications, 1985. (Musical score.)

Review of Chrysogonus Waddell, *The Twelfth-Century Cistercian Hymnal: Cistercian Studies*, 20 (1985), 772–73.

"The Cividale *Planctus Mariae*: From Manuscript to Modern Performing Edition," *Fifteenth Century Studies*, 13 (1988), 581–95.

(Editor.) *Holy Week and Easter Ceremonies and Dramas from Medieval Sweden*. Kalamazoo: Medieval Institute Publications, 1990.

*St. Martin's Mass*. Kalamazoo: St. Martin of Tours Church, 1990.

Review of Karol Berger, *Musica ficta: Theories of Accidental Inflections in Vocal Polyphony from Marchetto da Padova to Gioseffo Zarlino: Fifteenth Century Studies*, 18 (1991), 357–61.

"Another Manuscript of the *Ordo Virtutum* of Hildegard von Bingen," *Early Drama, Art, and Music Review*, 13 (1991), 36–40.

(Editor.) *The* Ordo Virtutum *of Hildegard of Bingen: Critical Studies*. Kalamazoo: Medieval Institute Publications, 1992.

"Music and Performance: Hildegard of Bingen's *Ordo Virtutum*." In *The* Ordo Virtutum *of Hildegard of Bingen* (1992), pp. 1–29 (see above).

Review of Sabina Flanagan, *Hildegard of Bingen: A Visionary Life: Mystics Quarterly*, 19 (1993), 84–86.

# 1. Pange Lingua

Venantius Fortunatus

Pan - ge lin - gua glo - ri - o - si Cor - por - ris my - ste - ri - um____:

San - gui - nis - que pre - ti - o - si, Quem in mun - di pre - ti - um___: Fruc - tus ven - tris

ge - ne - ro - si: Rex e - ffu - dit___ gen - ti - um. No - bis da - tus no - bis na - tus:

Ex___ in - tac - ta Vir - gi - ne___: Et in mun - do con - ver - sa - tus: Spar - so ver - bi

se - mi - ne_: Su - i mo - ros in - co - la - tus: Mi - ro clau - sit___ or - di - ne. In su - pre - me

noc - te ce - ne: Re - cum - bens cum fra - tri - bus___ : Ob - ser - va - ta le - ge

ple - ne Ci - bis in le - ga - li - bus_: Ci - bum tur - be du - o - de - ne: Se - dat su - is___

ma - ni - bus. Ver - bum ca - ro, pa - nem re___ rum ver - bo car - nem

46 e - ffi - cit_____: Fit - que san - guis Chri - sti me - rum: Et si sen - sus de - fi - cit_____

53 Ad fir - man - dum cor sin - ce - rum so - la fi - des_____ suf - fi - cit. Tan - tum er - go

60 sa - cra - men - tum: Ve - ne - re - mur cer - nu - i_____: Et an - ti - quam do - cu - men - tum:

65 no - ro ce - dat vi - tu - i_____: Pres - tet fi - des su - pple - men - tum: sen - su - um

72 de - fec - tu - i, Ge - ni - to - ri, ge - ni - to - que Laus et ju - bi-

77 la - ti - o_____: sa - lus, ho - nor, vir - tus quo - que Sit et

83 be - ne - dic - ti - o___: pro - ce - den - ti ab u - tro - que com - por sit lau - da - ti - o. A - men_____.

2

# 2. Salve festa dies

Sal - ve fes - ta di - es to - to ve - ne-ra - bi - lis e - vo qua

de - us ec - cle - si-am di - cat ho - no - re su - um.

Repeat "Salve festa dies" after each stanza

Ec - ce di - es lae - ta, post tris - ti - a tar - ta - ra spre - ta

Gra - ti - a su - cce - dit, per - di - ta vi - ta re - dit.

Hoc cor - pus Chris - ti sal - vans de fu - ne - re tris - ti

Ma - nna fi - gu - ra - rit, li - te - ra pris - ca ca - nit.

Hoc ver - bum pa - tris cae - lis for - ma - tor et or - bis

3

Cum pa - tre cunc - ta cre - at et de - i - ta - te be - at.

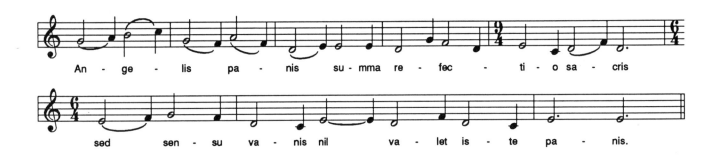

An - ge - lis pa - nis su - mma re - fec - ti - o sa - cris

sed sen - su va - nis nil va - let is - te pa - nis.

Hoc cor - pus ve - rum fir - mans pri - mor - di - a re - rum

In - fe - ra con - fre - git at - que re - demp - ta re - git.

Lau - dem com - pla - cu - it car - nem si - ne se - mi-

ne sump - sit, Vir - gi - nis et ma - tris vis - ce - ra sa - cra re - plet.

Repeat Salve festa dies

# 3. Alma redemptoris mater

# 4. Symphonia Virginum

Hildegard of Bingen

1. O dul - cis - si - me a - ma - tor o dul - cis - si - me am-

ple_____ xa - tor, ad - ju - va nos cu - sto - di-

re vir - gi - ni - ta - tem no - stram. 2. Nos su-

mus or - tae in pul - ve - re, he_____

_____ u, he_____ u, et in cri - mi - ne A_____

_____ dae. Val - de du - rum est con - tra-

di - ce - re quod ha - bet qu - stus po-

mi. Tu e - ri - ge nos, Sal - va - tor, Chri - ste.

3. Nos de - si - de - ra - mus ar - den - ter te se - qui.

O quam gra - ve no - bis mi - se - ris

est te im - ma - cu - la - tum et in - no - cen - tem Re - gem An -

ge - lo - rum i mi ta - ri. 4. Ta

men con - fi - di - mus in te, quod tu de - si - de - res gem -

qui mam re - re - re in pu - tre - di - ne. 5. Nunc ad -

vo - ca - mus te Spon - sum et con - so - la - to -

rem, qui nos re - de - mi - sti in cru

ce. 6. In tu - o san - gui - ne co -

pu - la - tae su - mus ti - bi cum de - spon - sa - ti - o -

ne, re - pu - di - an - tes vi - rum et e - li - gen - tes

te, Fi - li - um De_____ i_____. 7. O pul - cher - ri -

ma for_____ ma, O su - a - vis -

si - mus o_____ dor de - si - de - ra - bi - li -

um de - li - ci - a_____

_____ rum sem - per su - spi - ra - mus post

te in la - cri - ma - bi - li e - xi - li - o, quan -

do te vi - de - a - mus et te - cum

ma - ne - a - mus! 8. Nos su - mus in mun - do

et tu in men - te no_____ stra et am-

plec - ti - mur te in cor - de, qua - si

ha - be - a - mus te prae_____ sen-

tem. 9. Tu for - tis - si - mus le_____ o ru - pi - sti

cae - lum, de - scen - dens in au - lam Vir - gi-

____ nis_____ , et de - stru - xi - sti mor-

tem ae - di - fi - cans vi - tam in au - re - a

ci - vi - ta - te. 10. Da no - bis so - ci - e - ta - tem cum_____

9

\_\_ ll_____ la, et per - ma - ne - re in te o dul - cis - si-

me Spon - se, qui ab - stra - xi - sti nos de fau - ci-

bus Di - a - bo - li_____, pri - mum pa - ren_____

tem no - strum se - du_____ cen - tis.

# 5. Symphonia Viduarum

Hildegard of Bingen

O Pa - ter om - ni - um et o Rex et Im-

pe - ra - tor gen - ti - um, qui con - sti - tu - i - sti

nos in co - sta pri___ mae ma - tris, quae con - stru-

xit no - bis ma - gnum ca - sum de - rum - nae,___ et

nos se - cu - tae su - mus il - lam in pro - pri - a

cau - sa in e - xi - li - o, so - ci - an - tes nos il - li-

us do - lo - ri___. 2. O tu no - bi - lis - si - me Ge - ni-

___ tor, per sum - mum stu - di - um cur - ri-

11

mus ad te, et per di - lec - tis - si mam at - que per

dul - cis - si - mam poe - ni - ten - ti - am, quae no - bis

per - te ve - nit_____, an - he - la - mus ad te, et post do-

lo - rem no - strum de - vo - tis - si - me am

plec - ti - mur te. 3. O glo - ri - o - sis - si - me et

o pul - cher - ri - me Chri_____ste, qui es re - sur-

rec - ti - o vi - tae, nos re - li - qui - mus prop - ter te fer - ti-

lem a - ma - to - rem con - junc - ti - o_____nis, et

com - pre_____hen - di - mus te in su - per_____

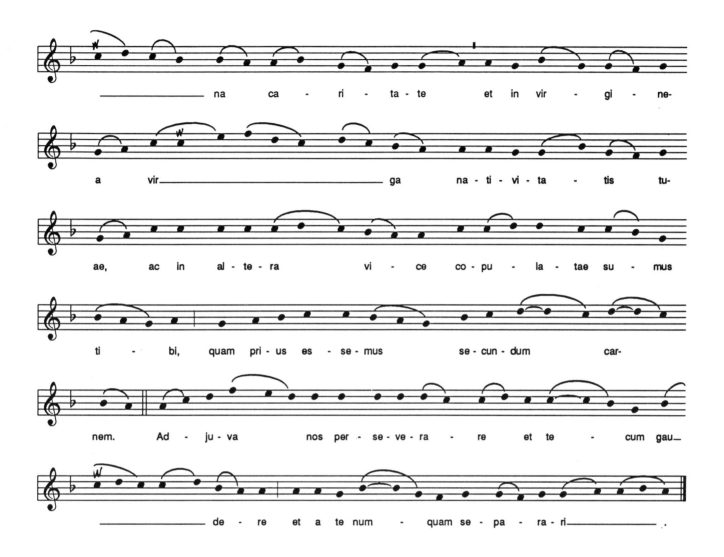

_____ na ca - ri - ta - te et in vir - gi - ne-

a vir_____ ga na - ti - vi - ta - tis tu-

ae, ac in al - te - ra vi - ce co - pu - la - tae su - mus

ti - bi, quam pri - us es - se - mus se - cun - dum car-

nem. Ad - ju - va nos per - se - ve - ra - re et te - cum gau\_

_____ de - re et a te num - quam se - pa - ra - ri_____ .

# 6. Maria muoter reinû maît

Ma - ri - a muo - ter rei - nû maît. Er - barm dich
ü - ber die cri - sten - hait. Er - barm dich ü - ber di - nû
kint dî noch in die - sem el - lind sint. Ma-
ri - a muo - ter gna - de vol du kanst und mahst uns
ghel - fen wol ver - lih uns ânn gne - di - gen dot. Und
bhôtt uns da vor al - ler not. Er - wirb uns
daz er uns los von
huld umm di - nes kint dez rich niem - mer dhain end
al - ler not und bhôt - te vor dem gâ - ben tot.

14

# 7. Nu tret herzuo der höffen welle

Nu tret her-zuo der höf - fen wel-le. Flie-hen von die hais - sum

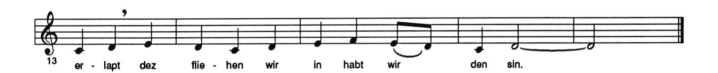

hel-le. Lu - ci-fer ist bos ge - sel-le. Wen er be - hapt mit bech

er - lapt dez flie-hen wir in habt wir den sin.

# 8. Wainent tögen mit den ougen

Wai - nent tö - gen mit den ou - gen habt in her - czen cri - stes smer - cen

slaht ûch ser durch cri - stes e - re daz ist uns fûr die sün - de gut

dez hilf uns lie - ber her - re got Je - sus wart ge - lasst mit gal - le.

16

# 9. Ad mortem festinamus

Ad mor - tem fe - sti - na - mus pec - ca - re de - si -
sta - mus pec - ca - re de - si - sta - mus Scri - be -
re pro - pro - su - i de con - tem - ptu mun - da - no
ut de - gen - tes se - cu - li non mul - cen - tur in va -
no iam est ho - ra sur - ge - re a somp - no mor - tis
pra - vo A somp - no mor - tis pra - vo. Ad mor -
tem fes - ti - na - mus pec - ca - re de - si - sta - mus pec -
ca - ra de - si - sta - mus Vi - ta bre - vis in bre - vi -
ter in bre - vi fi - ni - e - tur mors ve - nit ve -
lo - ci - ter qui ne - mi - nem ve - re - tur om - ni -
a mors pe - ri - mit et nul - li mi - se - re - tur, et

nul - li mi - se - re - tur. Ad mor - tem fes - ti - na-

mus pec - ca - re de - si - sta - mus, pec - ca - re de - si-

sta - mus. Ni con - ver sus su - er is et si - cut

pu - er fac - tus et vi - tam mu - tau - er - is in

mel - i - or - es ac - tus in tra - re non po - te-

ris req - num de - i be - a - tus. Ad mor - tem fes-

ti - na - mus pec - ca - re des - i - sta - mus, pec - ca - re

des - i - sta - mus: Tu - ba cum fon ve - rit di-

es - e - rit ex - tre - ma et ju - dex ad - ve - ne-

rit vo - ca - bit sem - pi - ter - na e - lec - tos in

pa - tri - a pre - sci - tos ad in - fer - na, pre - sci - tos

ad in - fer - na. Ad mor - tem fes - ti - na - mus pec-

ca - re des - i - sta - mus, pe - ca - re des - i - sta-

mus: Quam fe - li - ces fu - e - rit qui cum chris - to reg-

na - bunt fa - ci - e ad fa - ci - em fic cum

spec - ta - bunt sanc - tus sanc - tus do - mi - nus Sa-

ba - oth cun - cla - ma - bunt, Sa - ba - oth con - cla - ma-

bunt. Ad mor - tem fes - ti - na - mus pec - ca - re des - i-

sta - mus, pec - ca - re des - i - sta - mus: Et quam

tris - tes - fu - e - rint qui e - ter - ne pe - ri - bunt

pe - ne non de - fi - ci - ent non prop - ter has o - bi-

bunt he - u he - u mi - se - ri nun - quam in - de ex-

i - bunt nun - quam in - de ex - i - bunt. Ad mor-

tem fes - ti - na - mus pec - ca - re de - si - sta - mus, pec-

19

ca - re de - si - sta - mus: Cunc - ti re - ges se - cu-

li et in mun - do mag - na - tes ad - ven tant ec-

cle - si - am om - nes - que po - tes - ta - tes fi - ant

ve - lut par - vu - li di - mi - tant va - ni - ta - tes, di-

mi - tant va - ni - ta - tes. Ad mor - tem fes - ti - na-

mus pec - ca - re de - si - sta - mus, pec - ca - re de - si-

sta - mus: He - u fra - tres ka - ris - si - mi si dig - ne

con - tem - ple - mus pas - si - o - nem do - mi - ni a-

ma - re et si fle - mus ut pu - pil - lam oc - cu-

li fer - va - bit ne pec - ce - mus, fer - va - bit ne pec-

ce - mus. Ad mor - tem fes - ti - na - mus pec - ca - re

de - si - sta - mus, pec - ca - re de - si - sta - mus:

Al - ma vir - go vir - gi - num in ce - lis co - ro - na-
ta a - pud tu - um fi - li - um fis no - bis ad - vo-
ca - ta Et post hoc ex - i - li - um oc - cur - rens
me - di - a - ta, oc - cur - rens me - di - a - ta.
Ad mor - tem fe - sti - na mus pec - ca - re de - si-
sta - mus pec - ca - re de - si - sta - mus

# 10. Stella splendens in monte

1. Stel - la splen - dens in mon_____ te
2. Ip - sum in - gre - di - un_____ tur,

Ut so - lis ra - di - um    Mi - ra - cu - lis ser - ra_____ to,
Ut cer - nunt o - cu - li    Et    in - de re - ver - tun_____ tur

Ex - au - di po - pu_____ lum.    3. Con - cur - rent u - ni - ver - si
Gra - ci - is re - ple_____ ti.

Gau - den - tes po - pu - li    Di - vi - tes et e - ge_____ ni

D.C.

Gran - des et par - vu - li,

23

# 11. Rosa rorans

Nils Hermansson

Ro - sa ro - rans bo - ni - ta - tem, stel - la stil - lans

cla - ri - ta - tem, Bir - git - ta vas gra - ti - ae.

Ro___ ra cae - li - pi - e - ta - tem, stil - la

vi - tae pu - ri - ta - tem in val - lem mi - se - ri - ae.

# 12. Gloria

# 13. Aetas carmen melodiae

# 14. Das Kyrie

Ky - ri - e, Gott Va - ter in E - wig - keit,

gross ist dein Barm - her - zig - keit, al - ler Ding ein Schöp - fer und Re -

gie - rer; e - le - i - son, e - le - i - son!

Chri_____ste, al - ler Welt Trost, uns Sün -

30

der al - lein hast er - löst. O Je - su, Got - tes Sohn,

un - ser Mitt - ler bist in dem höch - sten Thron, zu dir schrei - en

wir aus Her - zens be - gier: e - le - i - son, e - le - i -

son. Ky - ri - e, Gott hei - li - ger

Geist, tröst, stärk uns im Glau - ben al - ler - meist, dass wir am

letz - ten End fröh - lich ab - schei - den aus die - sem E - lend;

e - le - i - son, e - le - i - son! A - men.

# 15. Ad arma

Isabella Leonarda

33

35

37

spi - ri-tus     ò  spi - ri-tus     re - bel - les     ve - ni-te ve-ni -

de - les  ser - vi - te  in   ar - tes  re - bel - les  ad   ar - ma ve - ni  -  te      ve -

te            ve - ni - te                                    Ca - dit

ni - te ve - ni - te                ve - ni - te

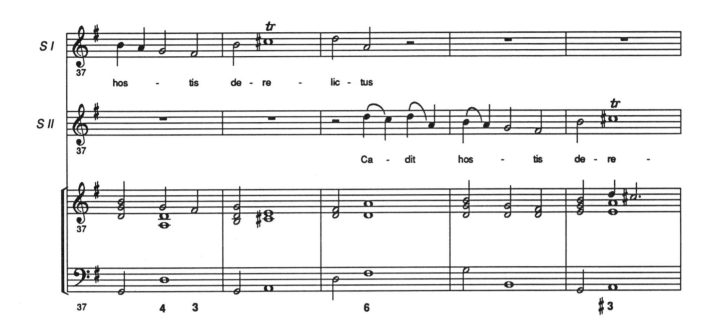

hos - tis de - re - lic - tus

Ca - dit hos - tis de - re -

4   3        6        #3

et bel - la

lic - tus        et bel - la

#5

39

trix tri - um - phat, et bel - la

trix tri - um - phat, et bel -

trix tri - um -

la trix tri - um -

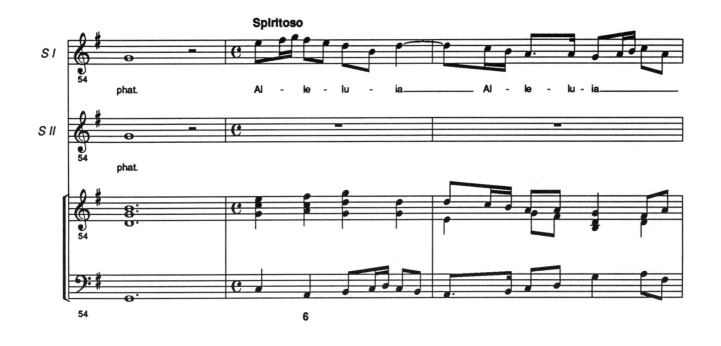

41

43

44

45

# 16. Laetatus sum

Isabella Leonarda

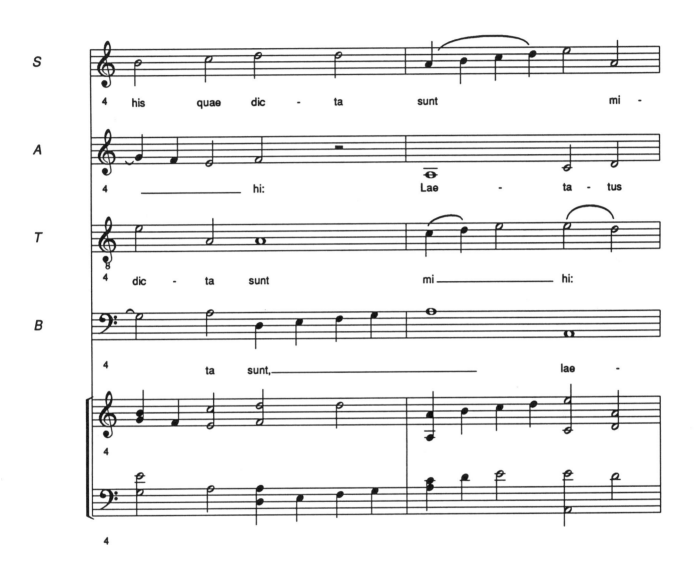

47

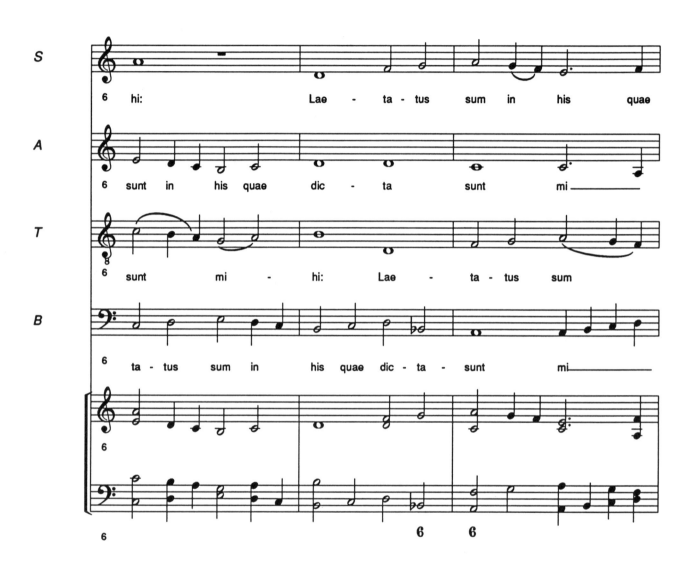

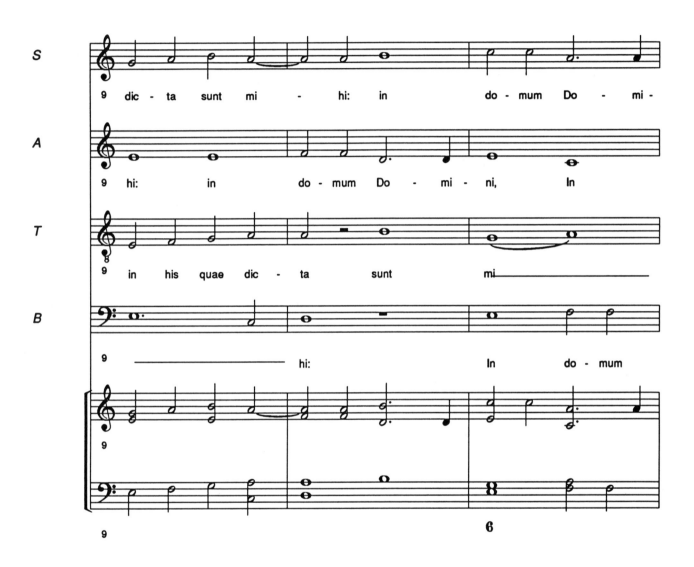

49

51

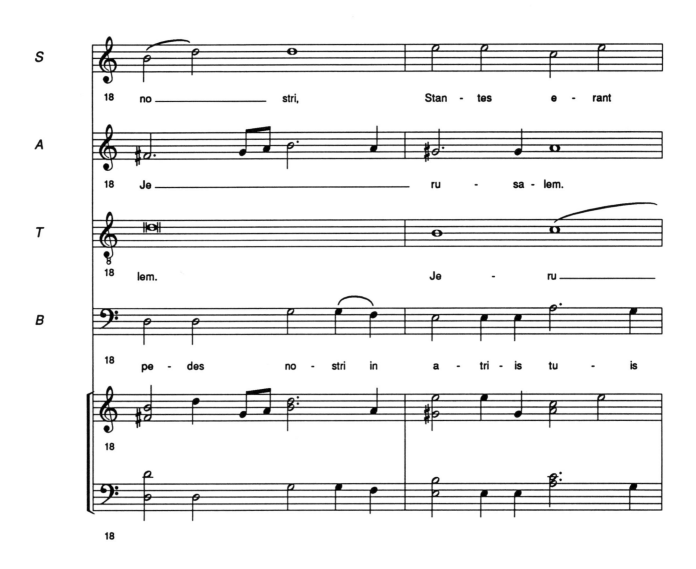

54

56

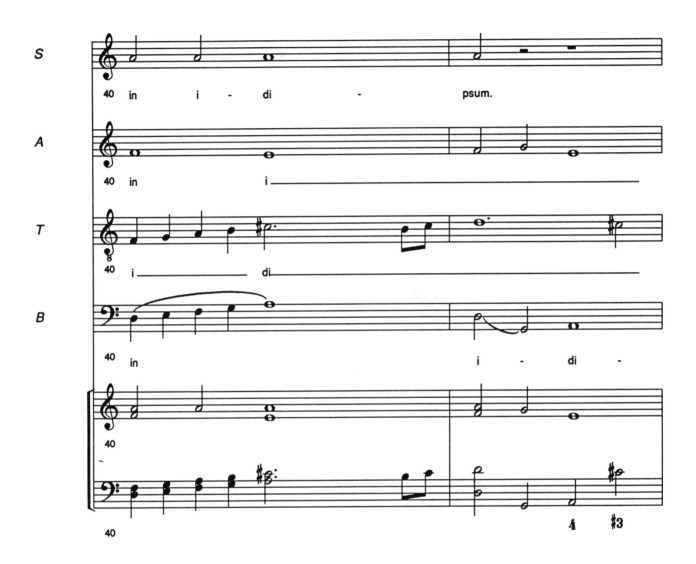

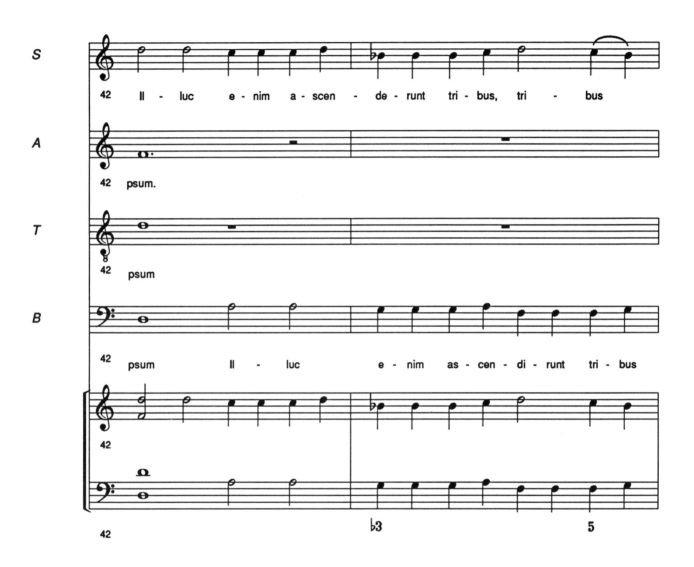

62

63

64

69

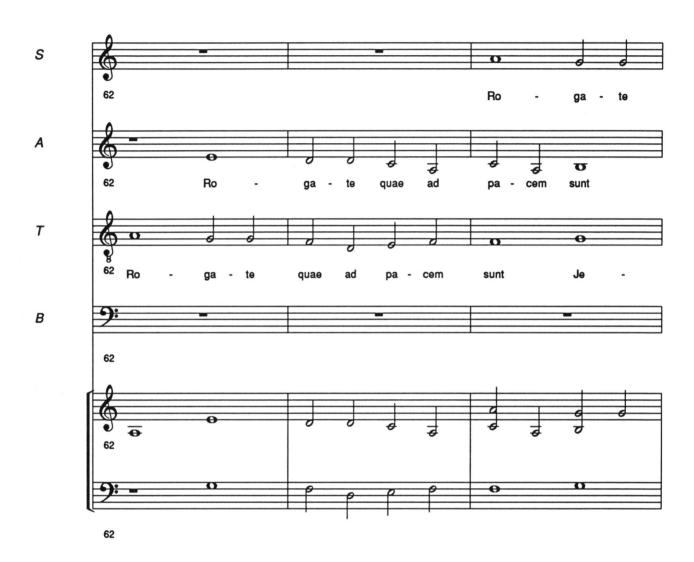

70

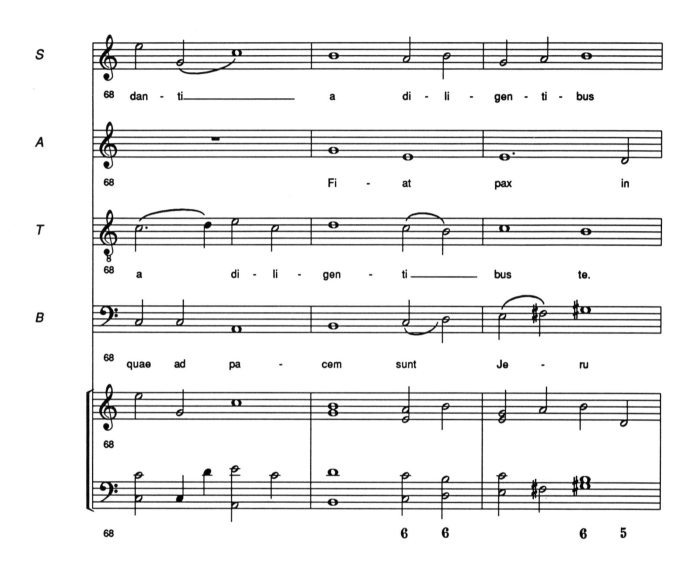

S: dan - ti_____ a  di - li - gen - ti - bus

A: Fi - at  pax  in

T: a  di - li - gen - ti_____ bus  te.

B: quae ad pa - cem sunt  Je - ru

6  6      6  5

72

73

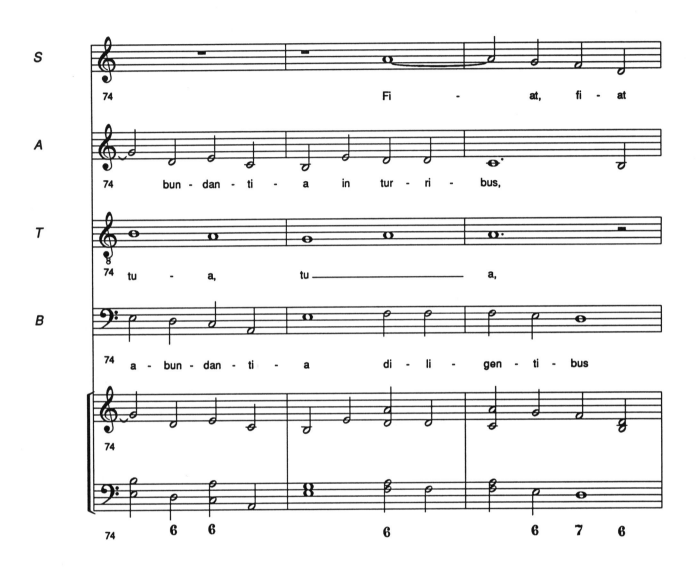

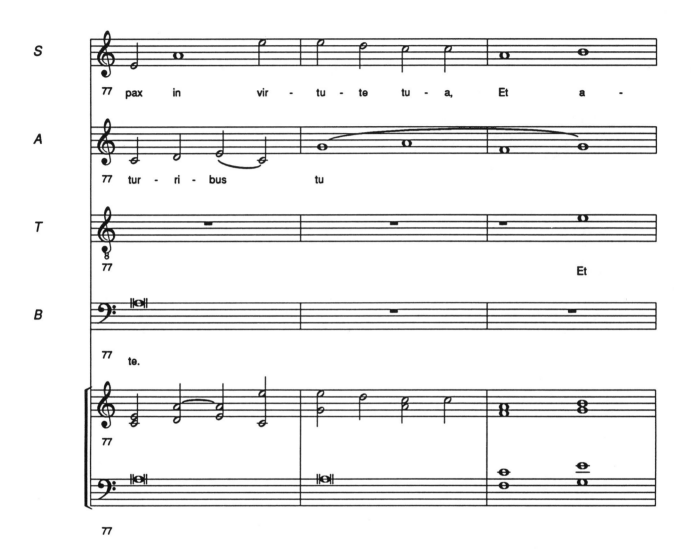

75

77

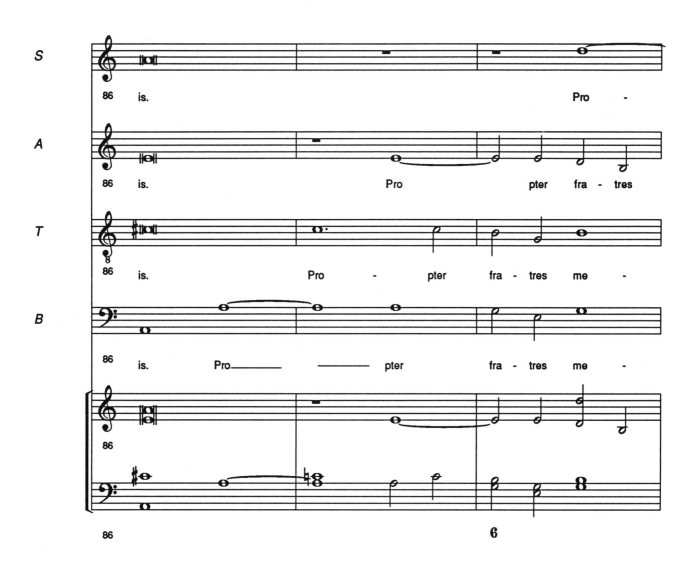

S 89 pter fra - tres me - os et pro - xi - mos

A 89 me os et pro - xi - mos

T 89 os. Pro — pter fra - tres me - os et

B 89 os. Pro - pter fra - tres me - os et

89

80

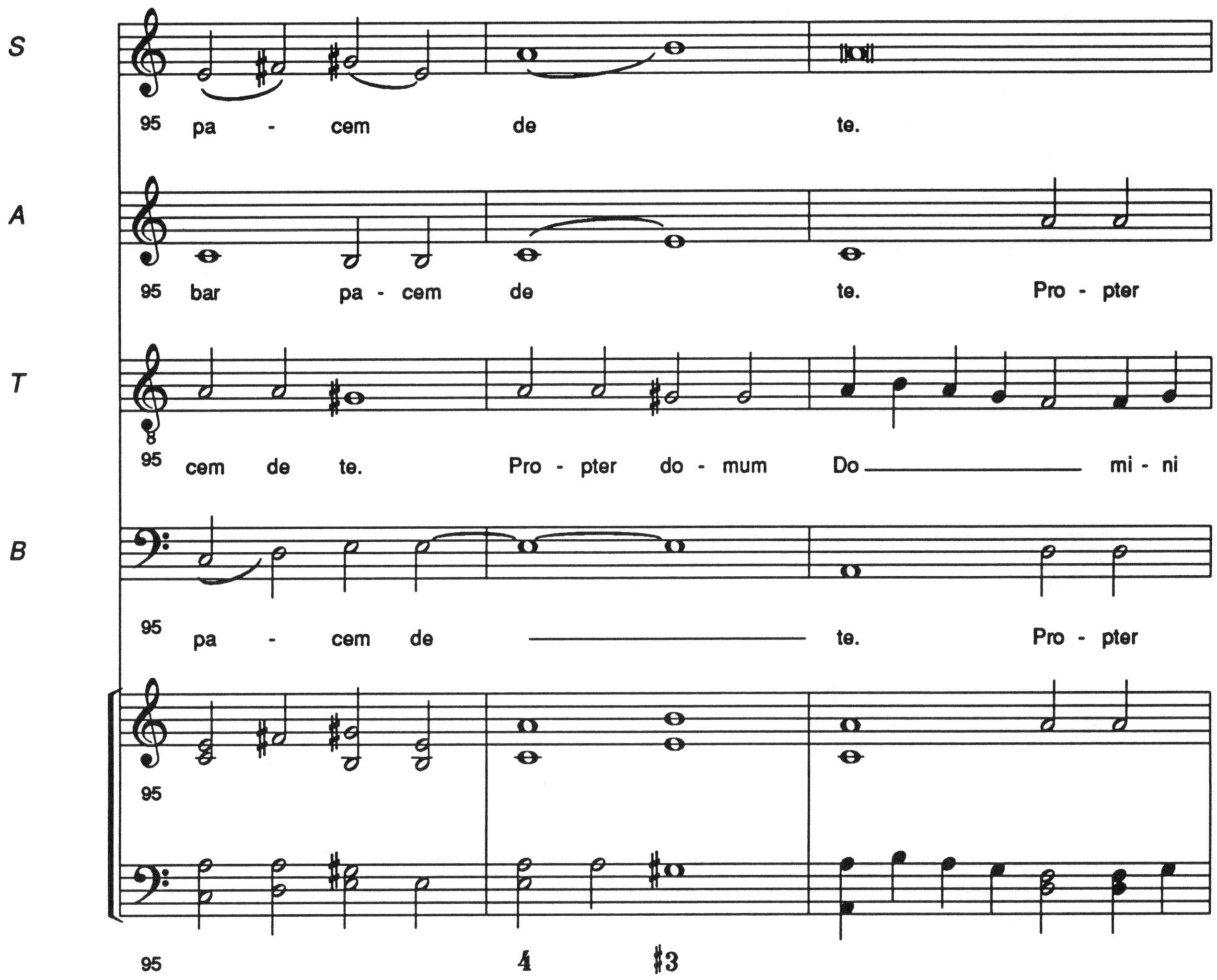
S
95 pa - cem de te.
A
95 bar pa - cem de te. Pro - pter
T
95 cem de te. Pro - pter do - mum Do mi - ni
B
95 pa - cem de te. Pro - pter
95
95 4 ♯3

S

**98**

Pro - pter

A

**98** do - mum Do _____ _ mi - ni De -

T

**98** De - i no - stri,

B

**98** do - mum Do _____ — mi - ni De -

**98**

82

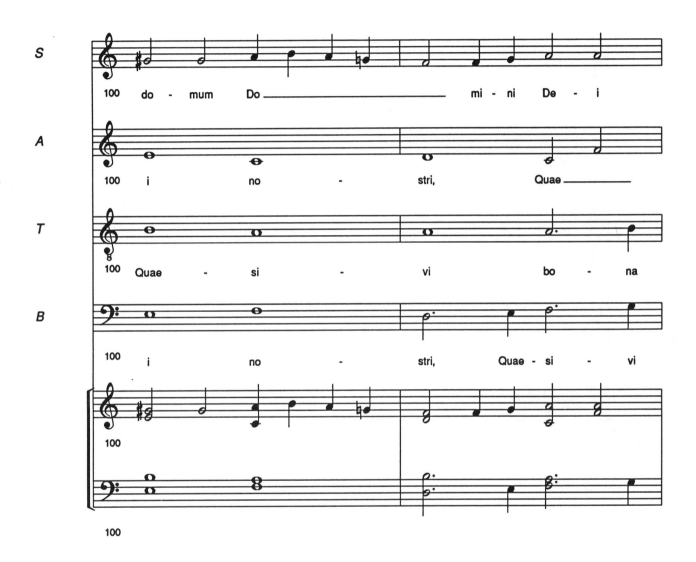

83

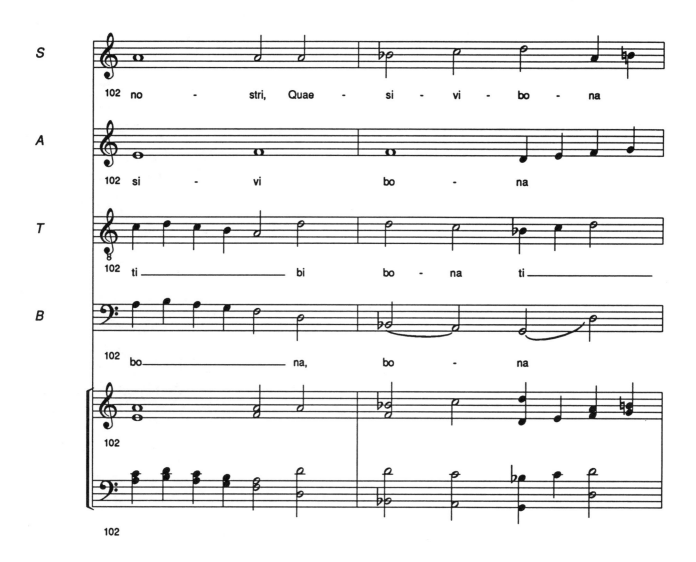

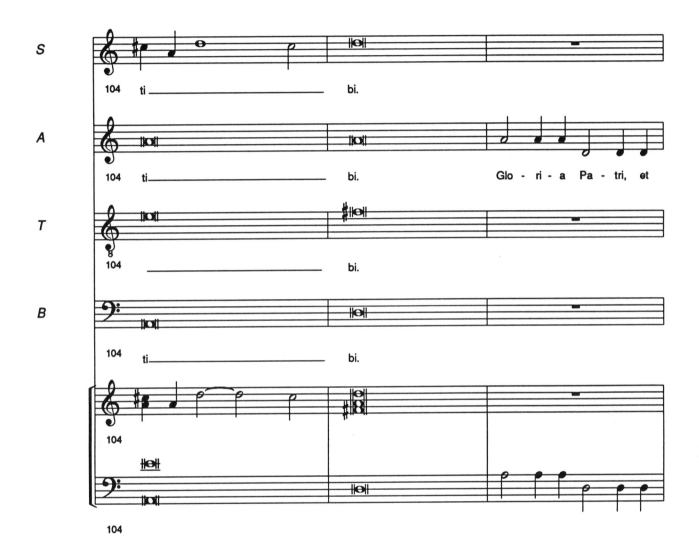

85

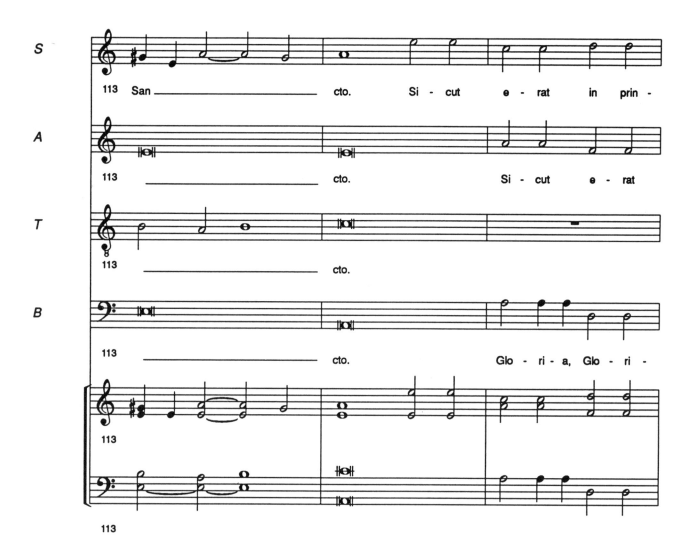

89

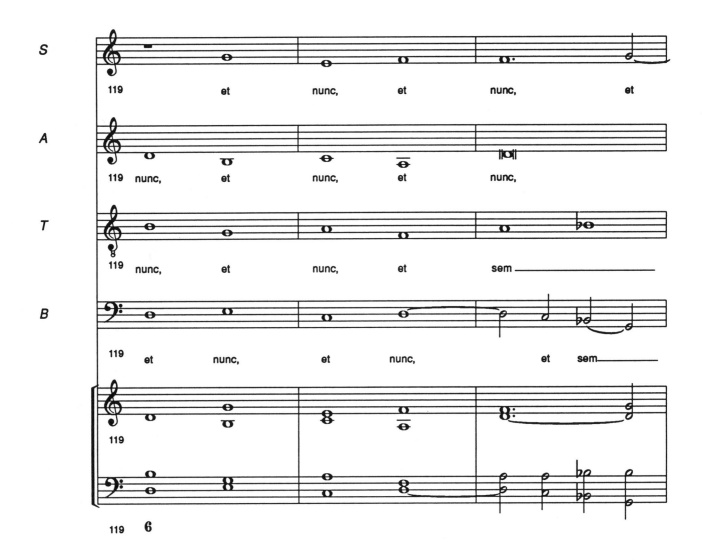

92

93

94

S

134 sae - cu - la sae - cu - lo _____

A

134 lo _____ rum.

T

134 rum. A _____

B

134 rum. A _____

134

134

S

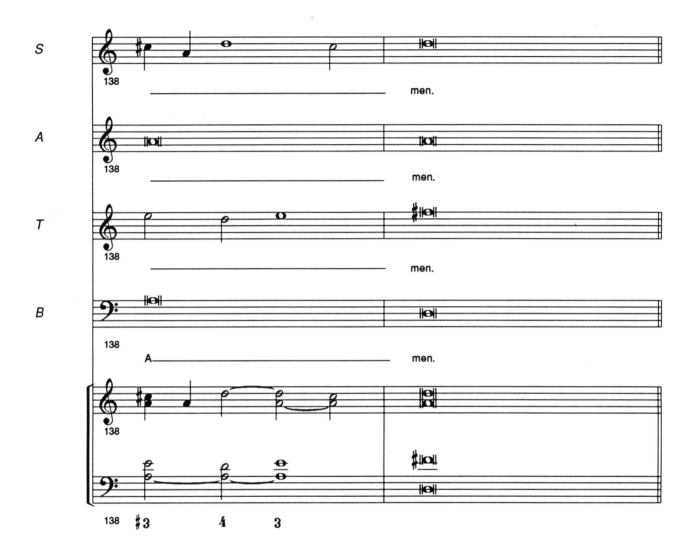

men.

A

men.

T

men.

B

A_____ men.

138   ♯3        4        3

97

# Notes on the Music
# and Translations

**1. Pange lingua.** Hymn. Text by Venantius Fortunatus (c.540–c.600) celebrating the gift of a fragment of the true cross given by the Byzantine Emperor Justinian II to Radegund in 569. The version presented here is from a Sarum service book.

*Praise, O tongue, the mystery of the glorious body, and of the precious blood which the King (the fruit of a noble womb) shed in the world for the people's redemption.*

*Given to us, born to us, from the undefiled Virgin, and dwelling on earth, he finished in a wondrous way his temporary sojourn after the seed of the Word was sown.*

*On the night of the Last Supper, while reclining with the brethren, he offered himself as food to the restless twelve.*

*The Word made flesh, he made bread to be the true flesh by the Word; and pure wine he made to be the blood of Christ.*

*And if understanding fails, then faith alone is enough to bolster a pure heart.*

*Let us, therefore, humbly venerate such a sacrament. And let the old ritual give way to the new rite. Let consummate faith make up for the deficiency of understanding.*

*Let praise, jubilation, salvation, honor, power, and blessing be to the Father and to the Son, and commendation be to the one proceeding from them both.*

**2. Salve festa dies.** Sarum processional hymn. The first line only is by Fortunatus.

*Hail, festival day, on which God commands his Church to honor him throughout all ages.*

*Behold the happy day; after hellish grief has been spurned, grace draws near, vitality follows. Hail, etc.*

*This is the body of Christ, relief from deadly grief; manna foretells it, the ancient psalm sings of it. Hail, etc.*

*This is the Word of the Father, maker of heaven and earth; with the Father he makes everything and in the Godhead blesses it. Hail, etc.*

*The bread of angels is the mightiest holy sustenance, but by the senses it counts as nothing. Hail, etc.*

*This true body, enclosing all things from the beginning, conquered hell and administered redemption. Hail, etc.*

*It deserves praise and has taken on flesh without seed; it swells the holy flesh of the Virgin and Mother. Hail, etc.*

**3. Alma redemptoris mater.** Antiphon, formerly attributed to Hermannus Contractus (Herman the Lame) (1013–54) of Reichenau. Sarum version, which differs slightly from continental examples. This antiphon was sung by the "litel clergeon" in Chaucer's Prioress' Tale. It was included in the first program presented by the Society for Old Music on 17 March 1966.

*Nurturing mother of the redeemer, who for souls is the open portal of heaven, and who is the star of the sea, help the fallen to arise.*

*You who as a virgin before as after, with nature marveling, gave birth to your Creator, receiving that "Hail" from the mouth of Gabriel, have mercy upon sinners.*

**4. Symphonia Virginum.** By Hildegard of Bingen (1098–1179). Her musical compositions, which are now much admired, were designed for use in her abbey at Rupertsberg near the Rhine. This song was sung by a choir of virgins, while the next item was to be sung by a choir of widows.

*O sweetest lover, O you sweetest embracer, help us guard our virginity.*

*We are born from dust, woe, woe, and from Adam's crime. It is hard to contradict that which tastes of the apple.*

*Christ, Savior, make us upright. We ardently desire to follow you. O how heavy upon us is the distress, to imitate the pure and innocent King of Angels.*

*Still we trust in you, such that you desire to seek a jewel amid rottenness.*

*Now we beseech you, the Bridegroom and consoler, who redeemed us on the cross.*

*We are joined to you in your blood with promises repudiating carnal man since we have chosen you, the Son of God.*

*O most beautiful form, O most agreeable fragrance of desirable allurement, we yearn after you always in tearful exile. When shall we see you, and stay with you?*

*We are in the world, and you are in our thought, and*

*we enfold you in our heart as if we had you before us. You, mighty lion, broke open the heavens, coming down to a virgin's dwelling, conquering death, and establishing life in the golden city.*

*Give us companionship with [the Virgin] and allow us to be with you, O sweetest Bridegroom, who extracted us from the devil's jaws, the one who seduced our first parent.*

**5. Symphonia Viduarum.** Widows' song. By Hildegard of Bingen.

*O Father of all, and King and commander of the nations, who made us from the rib of the first mother, who set us up for a great fall; and we followed her in her exile, associating ourselves with her grief.*

*O you, most noble Creator, we follow you with the utmost zeal, and the most pleasant penitence that comes through you. We are sighing for you, and after our grief we most devotedly embrace you, O most glorious and beautiful Christ, you who are the resurrection into life.*

*Because of you we gave up child-producing love and embrace you in heavenly charity, and we as virgins are joined to you of virgin birth instead of to that which we would first have been according to carnality.*

*Help us to endure, to be glad with you, and never to depart from you.*

**6. Maria muoter reinû maît.** This item, which was recorded by the Swabian priest Hugo Spechtshart of Reutlingen, and the following two are *Geisslerlieder* or Flagellant Songs, sung during exercises designed to ward off the plague in the late fourteenth century.

*Mother Mary, unblemished maiden, be merciful to Christendom. Take pity on your children who are still in this misery.*

*Mother Mary, full of grace, come and help us.*

*Help us be well and grant us a merciful death, and keep us from all harm.*

*Gain us grace so we may attain your Son's kingdom. May he free us from all want and protect us from death.*

**7. Nu tret herzuo der höffen welle.**

*Now come hither the hopeful waves, fleeing from fiery hell.*

*Lucifer is an evil fellow. If he rewards us with a [fiery] cup, we will escape from it if we have the desire.*

**8. Wainent tögen mit den ougen.**

*Let your eyes cry tears and have Christ's pain in your heart.*

*Beat yourselves for the honor of Christ; this is good for your sins.*

*Grant us your help, dear Lord God; Jesus waits. Endure bitterness.*

**9. Ad mortem festinamus.** From the *Llibre Vermell* (14th century). A Dance of Death from Spain.

*We hasten toward death; let us stop sinning. I have resolved to write of contempt of the world so those living in the world will not in vain be charmed. Now is the hour to rise from the vicious sleep of death.*

*We hasten toward death; let us stop sinning. Brief life briefly will be ended in a brief time; death, which fears no one, comes quickly. Death destroys all things and pities none.*

*We hasten toward death; let us stop sinning. Unless you have been converted and become as a child and have changed your life toward better deeds, you will not blessedly enter the kingdom of God.*

*We hasten toward death; let us stop sinning. When the trumpet has sounded, that day will be the last, and the Judge will come; he will call out the chosen ones for heaven, the foreknown [evil ones] to hell.*

*We hasten toward death; let us stop sinning. How happy will they be who will reign with Christ: when they see him thus, face to face, "Holy, holy Lord, Sabaoth" they will cry.*

*We hasten toward death; let us stop sinning. And how sorrowful will be those who are lost forever. They will not die; not because of these will they die. Alas, alas, alas, pitiful ones; never will they be able to go forth.*

*We hasten toward death; let us stop sinning. Let all the kings of the earth and the earth's great ones come to the Church, and all powerful persons become like little children; let them lose their vanity.*

*We hasten toward death; let us stop sinning. Alas, dearest brothers, if we worthily contemplate the Passion of the Lord, and if we weep as the pupil of our eye, he will keep us from sin.*

*We hasten toward death; let us stop sinning. Kind Virgin of Virgins, crowned in the heavens, with your Son may you be an advocate for us, and after this exile, hastening to meet us, our mediator.*

**10. Stella splendens in monte.** A pilgrim song from the *Llibre Vermell.* This collection of musical material, from Montserrat in Spain, was designed to present songs appropriate for pilgrims and sufficiently popular for their taste.

*Star resplendent on the mountain as a darting ray of the wondrous sun.*

*They themselves entered that their eyes might perceive, and then turn back to the magnitude of your grace.*

*The people came all together, rejoicing, the rich and the poor, the great and the lowly.*

**11. Rosa rorans.** An antiphon for the feast of St. Birgitta, written by Nils Hermansson (d. 1391), Bishop of Linköping and St. Birgitta's friend. Transcribed from the square-note edition of Sister M. Patricia of Sankta Birgittas Kloster, Vadstena, Sweden. The antiphon is still sung daily by the nuns at Vadstena.

*Rose dripping goodness, star dropping brightness; Birgitta, conduit of grace, let fall the mercy of heaven, bedew with purity of life this valley of distress.*

**12. Gloria.** From the *Liber Cantus* (Uppsala, 1620), designed to restore more traditional music, in both Swedish and Latin, for the Mass for use in the Church of Sweden after a period of unpopular Protestantizing that began in 1595.

*Glory be to God in the highest, and peace and good will to his people on earth.*

*Lord God, we praise you, we worship you, we give you thanks; we praise you for your glory; we thank you for your great glory.*

*O Lord God, heavenly king, God, Father Almighty.*

*O Lord, Jesus Christ, only Son, who is seated at the right hand of the Father, Lamb of God, you who take away the sins of the world, have mercy on us.*

*You alone are the holy one, you alone are the Lord, you alone are the most high, Jesus Christ, with the Holy Spirit in the glory of God the Father. Amen.*

**13. Aetas carmen melodiae.** From *Piae Cantiones* (1582), a collection of songs for the Church year prepared by Theodoricus Petri. It represented the first collection of printed music in Scandinavia.

*The age sings a harmonious song of praise to the Messiah in a melody of praise; for worthy of honor is he who by his Passion placated the Father of all grace.*

**14. Das Kyrie.** When Martin Luther decided upon the replacement of the Latin Mass with a vernacular German Mass, one option that was provided was a set of metrical settings, including this metrical version of the Kyrie.

*Lord God, Father in eternity, great is your mercy; Creator and ruler of all things, have mercy, have mercy.*

*Christ, comfort of all the world, you alone have redeemed our sins. O Jesus, Son of God, you are our mediator on the highest throne; to you we cry from yearning hearts: have mercy, have mercy.*

*Lord God, Holy Spirit, comfort and strengthen us in belief so that we may depart gladly from this misery to the final end. Have mercy, have mercy.*

**15. Ad arma.** By Isabella Leonarda (1620–after 1700), a nun of the convent of St. Ursula in Novara, Italy, and a prolific and respected composer of her time.

*To arms, to arms, you rebellious spirits!*

*Ready the sapping artillery, engage the cruel enemy, serve in the [pacific] arts.*

*Come to arms!*

*The forsaken enemy perishes, and the lady warrior triumphs.*

*Alleluia, alleluia.*

**16. Laetatus sum.** A setting by Isabella Leonarda of Psalm 121 (122).

*I rejoiced at the things that were said to me: We shall go into the house of the Lord. Our feet were standing in thy courts, O Jerusalem. Jerusalem, which is built as a city, which is compact together. For thither did the tribes go up, the tribes of the Lord: the testimony of Israel, to praise the name of the Lord. Because their seats have sat in judgment, seats upon the house of David. Pray ye for the things that are for the peace of Jerusalem: and abundance for them that love thee. Let peace be in thy strength: and abundance in thy towers. For the sake of my brethren, and of my neighbors, I spoke peace of thee. Because of the house of the Lord our God, I have sought good things for thee. Glory to the Father, and to the Son, and to the Holy Spirit: as it was in the beginning, is now, and shall be forever. Amen.*